Girls' Cookbook

A selection of recipes
that are perfect for girls!

First published in 2011
LOVE FOOD is an imprint of Parragon Books Ltd

Parragon
Queen Street House
4 Queen Street
Bath BA1 1HE, UK

ISBN: 978-1-4454-3802-3

Printed in China

Design by Talking Design
New photography by Mike Cooper
New home economy by Lincoln Jefferson
New recipes by Rachel Carter
Introduction by Moira Butterfield

With a special thank you to Isabelle and Eloïse Merry.

Notes for the Reader
This book uses metric measurements. All spoon measurements are level:
teaspoons are assumed to be 5 ml, and tablespoons are assumed to
be 15 ml. Unless otherwise stated, milk is assumed to be full fat, eggs and
individual vegetables are medium. Pepper is freshly ground black pepper.

The times given are an approximate guide only. Preparation times differ
according to the techniques used by different people and the cooking times
may also vary from those given. Optional ingredients, variations or serving
suggestions have not been included in the calculations.

Recipes using raw or very lightly cooked eggs should be avoided by
infants, the elderly, pregnant women, convalescents and anyone suffering
from an illness. Pregnant and breastfeeding women are advised to avoid
eating peanuts and peanut products. Sufferers from nut allergies should
be aware that some of the ready-made ingredients used in the recipes
in this book may contain nuts. Always check the packaging before use.

Contents

Steps to yummy cooking

There are three magic secrets to cooking:

Cooking is lots of fun.

Cooking makes people happy.

Cooking is a great way to be creative.

Those are pretty powerful secrets, don't you think?

You'll have a great time trying out recipes. Your friends and family will love sharing the treats you make, and healthy food is good for everybody.

Get set:

Ask the adults in your home if it's okay to cook. These recipes are designed to be made together so you will need their help with difficult bits. Show them the recipe you want to try and ask them to explain any words or steps that you don't understand.

Read the recipe carefully. Before you start, you'll need to make sure you have all the right ingredients and the equipment you need.

Always wash your hands before you start. That way you won't pass on any dirt or germs in your food.

Wear an apron to keep your clothes clean. You'll want to put yummy food in your mouth, not down your front!

All about ovens:

You might need to heat up an oven for your cooking (or other hot appliances). Ask an adult to help you do this.

Electric ovens measure heat in Centigrade (°C) or Fahrenheit (°F). Gas ovens measure heat in Marks (Gas Mark 3, for example).

All three heat measurements are in this book, so choose the one that's right for your oven.

Weigh it up:

You'll need to weigh and measure your ingredients carefully, so that your food will cook properly and taste good.

Use a jug to measure liquids and a weighing machine for solid things.

Ask an adult to show you how to use the weighing machine you have at home.

The measurements in this book are metric.
g = gram
ml = millilitre (for liquids)

Know your spoons:

A teaspoon (tsp) is the littlest spoon, the kind you might use to stir a drink.

A tablespoon (tbsp) is the biggest spoon – a bit too big to eat with but perfect for cooking.

If a recipe says 'one teaspoon' or 'one tablespoon' it means a level spoonful, not a heaped spoonful.

Cook's rules:

Always use oven gloves if you need to pick up a hot dish or a tin. That way you won't burn your hands (or you can ask an adult to help you).

Make sure you don't leave a mess once you have finished. If you clean up, the chances are you'll get to cook again soon.

How to use this book:

If you see this symbol (!) it means you need to ask an adult for help. This could be because a hot oven, hob, electrical appliance, sharp knives or scissors are involved in the recipe preparation.

All the recipes have symbols to help you. Look out for:

Serves/Makes

Preparation time
(in minutes)

Cooking time
(in minutes)

After you have made a recipe you can mark it out of 10 using the heart that looks like this:

Follow the fairy's dotted path on the opposite page to check you are ready to start cooking ...

Read the recipe before you start.

Try to get all your ingredients ready.

Make sure you have the equipment ready – see over the page for things you might need.

Wash your hands, put on your apron and tie back your hair if it is long.

For successful results, take care when weighing and measuring your ingredients.

Now you're ready to cook something yummy!

Know your equipment

1. Saucepan
2. Frying pan
3. Oven gloves
4. Chopping board
5. Mixing bowl
6. Rolling pin
7. Cooling rack
8. Bun tin
9. Baking tray
10. Wooden spoon
11. Measuring cups
12. Spatula
13. Balloon whisk
14. Measuring jug
15. Scales
16. Sieve
17. Biscuit cutter
18. Grater
19. Knife

Bake the most delicious treats

Butterfly Cakes

Fizzy Pink Cupcakes

Strawberry Muffins

Chocolate Chip Cookies

Fairy Wands

Button Biscuits

Butterfly Cakes

The little butterfly wings look really pretty and you can have lots of fun decorating them with sprinkles.

10

What you need:

140 g unsalted butter, cut into
small pieces, softened
140 g golden caster sugar
½ tsp vanilla extract
2 large eggs, lightly beaten
140 g self-raising flour, sifted
1–2 tbsp milk sprinkles,
to decorate

Butter icing:
85 g unsalted butter,
softened
175 g icing sugar
1 tbsp orange juice

1. Preheat the oven to 180°C/350°F/Gas Mark 4. Line a bun tin with 12 paper cases.

2. Put the butter and sugar into a large bowl and whisk using an electric hand mixer until the mixture is pale and fluffy. Add the vanilla extract and 1 egg and whisk on a low speed.

3. Whisk in a spoonful of flour, then the second egg and the milk. Very gently, stir in the rest of the flour using a wooden spoon to make a smooth mixture.

4. Using a dessertspoon, spoon the mixture into the paper cases. Bake for 12–15 minutes, until risen and golden. Remove from the oven and leave the cupcakes to cool a little, then move to a wire rack.

5. When cool, slice off the top of each cupcake and cut in half to make 2 wings. For the butter icing, beat together the butter, icing sugar and orange juice in a medium bowl.

6. Place a spoonful of icing on top of each cupcake and decorate with sprinkles. Place the wings on top.

Step 2

Step 4

Step 6

Fizzy Pink Cupcakes

These cute cupcakes look just like a glass of fizzy pink lemonade.
Add a straw to the top and serve as a fun treat!

What you need:

115 g self-raising flour, sifted

¼ tsp baking powder

115 g unsalted butter, cut into small pieces, softened

115 g caster sugar

2 large eggs, lightly beaten

pink, white and red sprinkles, to decorate

10 pink drinking straws, cut to 8 cm long, to serve

Butter icing:

115 g unsalted butter, softened

225 g icing sugar

1 tbsp lemon juice

pink food colouring

1. Preheat the oven to 180°C/350°F/Gas mark 4. Line a bun tin with 10 paper cases.

2. Put the flour and baking powder into a large bowl. Add the butter, caster sugar and eggs and whisk using an electric hand mixer until the mixture is pale and fluffy.

3. Using a dessertspoon, spoon the mixture into the paper cases. Bake for 15–20 minutes, until risen and golden. Remove from the oven and leave the cupcakes to cool a little, then move to a wire rack.

4. For the butter icing, beat together the butter, icing sugar and lemon juice in a medium bowl. Stir in a little pink food colouring to give a pale pink colour.

5. Thickly swirl the icing over the tops of the cupcakes using a palette knife. Put the sprinkles on a plate, hold onto the paper cases and roll the cupcake edges in the sprinkles.

6. Push a straw into the top of the cupcakes to decorate.

Strawberry Muffins

It's not until you bite into these delicious muffins that you discover the secret strawberry jam filling inside.

What you need:

225 g plain flour

1 tsp baking powder

140 g golden caster sugar

100 ml milk

2 large eggs

140 g unsalted butter, melted

12 tsp strawberry jam

6 strawberries, halved, to decorate

Butter icing:

45 g unsalted butter, softened

85 g icing sugar

½ tsp vanilla extract

1–2 tsp milk

1. Preheat the oven to 200°C/400°F/Gas Mark 6. Line a muffin tin with 12 paper cases.

2. Sift the flour and baking powder into a large bowl. Stir in the caster sugar using a wooden spoon. Put the milk, eggs and melted butter in a jug and whisk together with a balloon whisk. Pour a little at a time into the bowl, stirring gently until mixed together well.

3. Spoon a heaped dessertspoon of the muffin mixture into each paper case, then add a teaspoonful of jam. Top with the rest of the muffin mixture.

4. Bake in the preheated oven for 20–25 minutes, until risen and golden. Remove the muffins from the oven and leave to cool a little, then move to a wire rack.

5. For the butter icing, beat together the butter, icing sugar, vanilla extract and milk in a medium bowl.

6. Place a spoonful of the butter icing on top of each muffin, then decorate with a strawberry half.

Step 2

Step 4

Step 6

Chocolate Chip Cookies

These yummy chocolate chip cookies taste best warm. They are so deliciou
you'll want to make them time and time again!

10

What you need:

125 g unsalted butter,
cut into small pieces

100 g soft brown sugar

2 tbsp golden syrup

1 tsp vanilla extract

175 g plain flour

pinch of salt

150 g milk chocolate,
cut into small chunks

1 egg, beaten

(!) 1. Preheat the oven to 180°C/350°F/Gas Mark 4. Line two baking trays with baking paper.

2. Place the butter and brown sugar in a large bowl and using a wooden spoon, stir until mixed together.

3. Add the golden syrup and vanilla extract and stir again until combined. Stir in the flour, salt, chocolate and egg and gently mix together to make a soft dough.

(!) 4. Spoon small amounts of the dough onto the baking trays, making sure you space them well apart, and bake in the preheated oven for 12–15 minutes until golden.

(!) 5. Remove the trays from the oven and leave the cookies to cool a little, then move to a wire rack to cool completely.

Step 2

Step 3

Step 4

Fairy Wands

Add a little magic to your cooking with these fantastic fairy wands.
You can decorate them to make each wand special!

10

What you need:

250 g plain flour, sifted, plus extra for dusting

100 g caster sugar

115 g cold butter, cut into small pieces

1 tbsp milk

12 ice-lolly sticks or wooden skewers

To decorate

1 egg white, lightly beaten

pink pearl sugar balls

pink edible glitter

1. Preheat the oven to 160°C/325°F/Gas Mark 3. Line 2 baking trays with baking paper.

2. Put the flour and sugar in a large bowl and mix together. Rub in the butter using your fingertips to make a soft buttery mixture. It should look like breadcrumbs.

3. Stir in the milk using a wooden spoon, then bring the mixture together with your hands to make a dough.

4. Lightly flour the work surface and rolling pin. Knead the dough gently until smooth, then roll out until it is about 5 mm thick. Use a heart-shaped cutter to stamp out 12 hearts and carefully put on the prepared baking trays.

5. Press a small wooden ice-lolly stick into each one and cover the 'handles' with foil so that they don't burn during cooking.

6. Bake in the preheated oven for 15–20 minutes, until pale and golden. Remove from the oven and leave the shortbread to cool a little, then move to a wire rack.

7. Brush the hearts with egg white, sprinkle the decorations of your choice over them and leave to cool.

Button Biscuits

These button-shaped biscuits can be threaded with coloured ribbons to make them look extra special.

10

What you need:

250 g plain flour, sifted, plus extra for dusting

25 g cornflour

75 g caster sugar

175 g unsalted butter cut into small pieces

1–2 tsp milk

thin ribbons, to decorate

(!) 1. Preheat the oven to 180°C/350°F/Gas Mark 4. Line 2 baking sheets with baking paper.

2. Put the flour, cornflour and caster sugar into a large bowl. Rub in the butter using your fingertips to make a soft buttery mixture. It should look like breadcrumbs.

3. Stir in the milk using a wooden spoon, then bring the mixture together with your hands to make a dough.

4. Lightly flour the work surface and rolling pin. Gently knead the dough until smooth, then roll out until it is about 5 mm thick.

5. Use a round cutter to stamp out 19 circles and carefully put on the prepared baking trays.

(!) 6. Use a skewer to make 4 holes in each biscuit so it looks like a button, turning the skewer to make the holes big enough to thread the ribbon through.

(!) 7. Bake in the preheated oven for 10–12 minutes, until pale and golden. Remove from the oven and leave the biscuits to cool a little, then move to a wire rack. When cool, thread the ribbons through the holes and tie the ends into a bow.

Step 2

Step 4

Step 5

Impress with everyday eats

Very Berry Pancakes

Perfect Porridge

Veggie Skewers

Super Stuffed Potatoes

Mighty Meatballs

Fantastic Fajitas

24

Very Berry Pancakes

Your family and friends will love these light American-style pancakes – they're so moreish that they'll disappear in seconds!

What you need:

150 g self-raising flour, sifted

2 tbsp caster sugar

1 large egg, lightly beaten

175 ml milk

3 tbsp thick natural yogurt, plus extra to serve

2 tbsp unsalted butter, for frying

275 g frozen mixed summer fruits, defrosted

maple syrup, to serve

1. Put the flour and sugar in a medium mixing bowl and stir until mixed together. Make a dip in the centre. Mix together the egg and milk in a jug.

2. Pour the milk mixture into the flour. Add the yogurt and stir with a wooden spoon until you have a smooth batter.

3. Melt a quarter of the butter in a large frying pan. Add 3 dessertspoonfuls of batter to make 3 pancakes, each one about 6 cm diameter.

4. Cook for 2 minutes until bubbles appear on the top and the underneath is golden. Flip each pancake over with a palette knife and cook for another minute.

5. Repeat with the rest of the batter to make about 16 pancakes. Add a little more butter when the pan looks dry.

6. Serve the pancakes with a large spoonful of fruit and yogurt and drizzle over the maple syrup.

Step 1

Step 3

Step 6

Perfect Porridge

Just the thing to warm you up on a cold winter's morning,
this creamy porridge is topped with a cinnamon apple purée, maple syrup
and pecan nuts.

10

What you need:

200 g whole porridge oats
800 ml milk
800 ml water
8 pecan nuts, to serve
(optional)
maple syrup, to serve

Cinnamon apple purée:
4 apples
1 tsp lemon juice
175 ml water
½–1 tsp ground cinnamon

1. For the purée, remove the skin from the apples using a vegetable peeler. Cut the apple into quarters, remove the core then cut into small pieces.

2. Put the apples, lemon juice, water and cinnamon in a small saucepan. Cover and simmer for 15 minutes until the apples are soft.

3. While the apple mixture is cooking, put the oats in a large saucepan with the milk and water and bring to the boil.

4. When the oat mixture is bubbling, reduce the heat to low, half cover the pan with a lid and simmer for 8 minutes, stirring frequently.

5. Mash the apple with a fork until mushy. Spoon the creamy porridge into 4 bowls then top each one with apple purée.

6. Add the pecans, if using, and pour a little of the maple syrup over. Arrange the nuts and syrup in a fun pattern.

Veggie Skewers

Use brightly coloured vegetables to create vibrant veggie skewers!
These skewers are so yummy that they'll brighten up any day.

10

What you need:

1 yellow and 1 red pepper,
seeded and cut into
small chunks

1 courgette, trimmed
and sliced

100 g button mushrooms,
wiped and halved

barbecue sauce,
to serve

Flavoured oil:

2 tbsp olive oil

1 tbsp clear honey

1 tbsp tomato ketchup

1 clove garlic, crushed

½ tsp dried mixed herbs

salt and pepper

1. For the flavoured oil, put the oil, honey, ketchup, garlic, herbs and salt and pepper into a small bowl and mix together.

2. Place the vegetables in a clean plastic food bag and pour in the flavoured oil. Seal the bag and turn it a few times to coat all the vegetables in the oil. Leave for 10 minutes.

3. Thread the vegetables onto 8 skewers, alternating the different colours.

4. Turn the grill to high or heat a griddle. Add the skewers and cook for about 8-10 minutes, turning regularly, until the vegetables are starting to soften.

5. Serve the skewers with the barbecue sauce.

Step 2

Step 3

Step 4

Super Stuffed Potatoes

These warm cheesy potatoes are the perfect treat for a delicious supper.
Serve them on their own or with some tasty fresh vegetables.

10

What you need:

4 medium-sized baking
potatoes, scrubbed

1 tbsp olive oil

150 g Cheddar cheese,
grated

25 g butter

50 ml milk

125 g ham, chopped

salt and pepper

1. Preheat the oven to 220°C/425°F/Gas Mark 7. Rub the potato skins with the olive oil using a piece of clean kitchen paper. Sprinkle the skins with a little salt.

2. Place the potatoes on a baking tray, pierce with a fork and bake in the preheated oven for 1 hour or until the potatoes are soft when pierced with the tip of a sharp knife.

3. Remove the potatoes from the oven, cut in half and allow to cool for 10–15 minutes.

4. Carefully scoop out the insides of the potatoes without breaking the skins, put the potato into a mixing bowl and mash well with a fork.

5. Add 100 g of the cheese, the butter, milk and ham and season with some salt and pepper.

6. Put the potato mixture back into the skins using a spoon and top with the remaining cheese. Place on a baking tray and put back in the oven for 10–15 minutes until the tops are golden.

Step 1

Step 4

Step 6

Mighty Meatballs

Everyone loves meatballs and these are no exception. They come in a rich tomato sauce and are served on a bed of swirly spaghetti.

10

What you need:

45 g crustless, day-old bread, broken into chunks

400 g lean beef mince

2 cloves garlic, crushed

1 large egg, lightly beaten

40 g Parmesan cheese, finely grated

flour, for coating

300 g dried spaghetti

salt and pepper

Tomato sauce:

2 tbsp olive oil

2 cloves garlic, crushed

2 tsp dried oregano

2 x 400 g cans chopped tomatoes

1 tbsp tomato purée

1 tsp sugar

1. Put the bread in a food processor and whizz until it makes breadcrumbs. Add the mince, garlic, egg, Parmesan cheese and salt and pepper.

2. Process the mince mixture until it comes together in a ball. Flour your hands, take small amounts of the mixture and roll into balls the size of walnuts. Leave to chill.

3. For the tomato sauce, heat the oil in a saucepan and add the garlic and oregano. Stir for 1 minute.

4. Add the chopped tomatoes, tomato purée and sugar. Bring to the boil, then reduce the heat and simmer for 8 minutes.

5. Carefully place the meatballs in the pan and spoon the sauce over them. Cover and simmer for 20 minutes, turning the meatballs occasionally.

6. Meanwhile, cook the spaghetti in a large pan of salted water, following the instructions on the packet. Drain and serve with the meatballs and sauce.

Fantastic Fajitas

Once you've made your yummy filling you can have fun making the fajitas. Make sure you wrap them tightly as you don't want your filling to fall out!

10

* plus marinating time

What you need:

grated rind and juice 1 lime
1 tsp sugar
1 tsp dried oregano
2 tsp smoked paprika
2 tbsp olive oil
350 g chicken breast fillets,
cut into bite-sized pieces
1 red onion, finely sliced
1 orange and 1 red pepper,
seeded and diced
85 g button mushrooms,
wiped and sliced

To serve:
8 tortilla wraps
grated Cheddar cheese
guacamole and sour cream
shredded iceberg lettuce

1. Put the lime rind and juice, sugar, oregano, paprika and half the olive oil in a large bowl and mix together.

2. Add the chicken and toss well to coat. Cover with cling film and place in the fridge for 1-2 hours to marinate.

3. Heat the remaining oil in a large frying pan and cook the marinated chicken for 4-5 minutes. Add the vegetables and continue to stir fry for a further 3–4 minutes, stirring regularly, until the chicken is thoroughly cooked.

4. Heat a non-stick frying pan or griddle pan, then add the tortillas, one at a time, and warm for 10 seconds on each side.

5. Spoon a little of the chicken filling onto each tortilla wrap. Add a little cheese, guacamole, sour cream and lettuce. Roll up each wrap tightly.

Step 1

Step 2

Step 5

Throw the most perfect party

Golden Nuggets

Pizza Party

Cute Mini Burgers

Hot Dogs & Chips

Maple Syrup Popcorn

Scrumptious S'mores

Golden Nuggets

These golden nuggets of breadcrumbs and chicken taste great and are delicious when dipped into tomato ketchup.

10

What you need:

4 tbsp plain flour
2 eggs, beaten
25 g Cheddar cheese, grated
125 g fresh breadcrumbs
400 g chicken breast fillets,
chopped into chunks
salt and pepper
tomato ketchup, to serve

1. Preheat the oven to 200°C/400°F/Gas Mark 6. Line a baking tray with baking paper.

2. Put the flour in a small bowl and season with some salt and pepper. Put the eggs in another small bowl and put the cheese and breadcrumbs in another small bowl.

3. Dip each chicken chunk first in the flour to coat lightly, then dip in the egg and finally in the cheesy breadcrumb mixture.

4. Place the chicken pieces on the prepared baking tray and cook for 22–25 minutes turning once until the coating is golden and the chicken is thoroughly cooked.

5. Serve immediately with tomato ketchup.

Step 2

Step 3

Step 4

Pizza Party

This makes 2 large pizzas – perfect for a party! Each quarter of the pizza has a different topping, which means that there is something for everyone.

2   20*   10–15

* plus time for bases to stand

What you need:

400 g strong white flour

1 tsp salt

7 g sachet easy-bake dried yeast

1 tbsp olive oil, plus extra for brushing

250 ml lukewarm water

2 x 150 g balls of mozzarella, torn into pieces

sliced pitted olives, ham slices, pineapple chunks, and sliced vegetables, for the topping

Tomato sauce:

1 tbsp olive oil

200 ml passata

2 tsp tomato purée

1 tsp dried oregano

1. Mix together the flour, salt and yeast in a large bowl. Make a dip in the centre and pour in the oil and water, then mix to make a soft dough.

2. Lightly flour the work surface and rolling pin, then knead the dough for 10 minutes, until smooth.

3. Divide the dough into 2 pieces and roll out to make 2 thin pizza bases. Put the pizza bases on two baking sheets and leave in a warm place for 20 minutes. Preheat the oven to 230°C/450°F/Gas Mark 8.

4. To make the tomato sauce, mix together the oil, passata, tomato purée and oregano in a small bowl. Spoon onto the bases and spread thinly over the pizza bases with the back of a dessertspoon.

5. Sprinkle the pizzas with the mozzarella and top each quarter with a different topping of your choice.

6. Brush the topping with oil and bake the pizzas for 10–15 minutes. Remove from the oven, then cut each pizza into 8 slices with a knife or pizza wheel.

Step 1

Step 2

Step 5

Cute Mini Burgers

Making your own burgers is lots of fun and they taste great too. These mini burgers are so cute that everyone at your party will love them!

What you need:

1 onion, finely grated
2 cloves garlic, crushed
500 g steak mince
1 tbsp herbes de provence
2 tbsp tomato ketchup
1 tbsp olive oil
75 g Cheddar cheese,
thinly sliced
salt and pepper

To serve:
mini burger rolls
gherkins, thinly sliced
salad leaves
tomato ketchup

1. Put the onion, garlic, mince, dried herbs, tomato ketchup, and salt and pepper in a large bowl and mix together with your hands until well combined.

2. Shape into 12 equal-sized small burgers.

3. Heat half the oil in a large frying pan and cook the first 6 burgers for about 4-5 minutes. Turn the burgers and cook for 2–3 minutes, then top with the cheese and continue cooking for another 2-3 minutes or so until the cheese is just starting to melt.

4. Check that the burgers are thoroughly cooked by piercing with the tip of a sharp knife. Any juices that run out should be clear. Cook the rest of the burgers in the same way.

5. Serve the burgers in the rolls, topped with the gherkins, salad leaves and tomato ketchup. Secure with a cocktail stick.

Step 1

Step 2

Step 5

Hot Dogs & Chips

These mini hotdogs make great party food and the chips are extra special as they are home-made sweet potato chips.

10

What you need:

4 sweet potatoes, peeled
and cut into thin chips
2 tbsp olive oil
8 mini hot dogs
salt and pepper
4 large hot dogs rolls and
tomato ketchup, to serve

1. Preheat the oven to 200°C/400°F/Gas Mark 6.
Line a baking tray with baking paper.

2. Put the sweet potato chips on the prepared
baking tray.

3. Pour a little oil over the chips and add some
salt and pepper. Use your hands to coat the chips
in the oil.

4. Place the chips in the preheated oven for
20–25 minutes until the chips are golden,
turning occasionally.

5. Meanwhile, cook hot dogs as it says on the
package instructions.

6. Cut each roll in half and place a mini hot dog in
each half with some tomato ketchup. Serve with
the sweet potato chips.

Step 2

Step 3

Step 6

Maple Syrup Popcorn

Great fun to make and very tasty to eat, popcorn is the perfect party snack. Serve it in a big bowl so everyone can tuck in!

10

What you need:

1–2 tbsp vegetable oil
75 g popping corn
1 tbsp butter
3 tbsp maple syrup
1 tbsp sesame seeds

(!) 1. Pour the oil into a saucepan and heat over a medium heat.

(!) 2. Carefully add the popcorn to the pan in an even layer and cover with a lid. A glass lid is best so you can see into the pan.

(!) 3. Cook the popcorn over a medium–low heat, shaking the pan occasionally, until the corn kernels pop.

(!) 4. Pour the popcorn into a large mixing bowl, taking out any kernels that have not popped.

(!) 5. Melt the butter in a small saucepan, then pour in the maple syrup. Bring to the boil, then remove from the heat and cool.

(!) 6. Pour the maple syrup sauce over the popcorn and add the sesame seeds. Stir to mix together.

Scrumptious S'mores

Make really delicious s'mores by sandwiching chocolate and marshmallows between two chocolate chip cookies.

10

What you need:

8 large chocolate chip cookies

8 marshmallows, sliced in half horizontally (or you could use mini marshmallows)

60 g milk chocolate, cut into small squares

1. Preheat the oven to 200°C/400°F/Gas Mark 6. Line a baking tray with baking paper.

2. Place four cookies on the prepared baking tray upside down and top with 4 pieces of marshmallow and a few pieces of chocolate.

3. Place another cookie, right side up, on top and press down lightly.

4. Place in the preheated oven for 6–8 minutes until the marshmallow is starting to ooze and the chocolate beginning to melt.

5. Put the s'mores on a pretty plate and serve warm.

Step 2

Step 3

Step 4

Make the yummiest desserts

Chocolate Mousse

Ice Cream Sundae

Meringue Clouds

My Own Apple Pie

Raspberry Jelly

Chocolate Mousse

Nothing could be more delicious to eat than chocolate mousse. Top with cream and pretty sprinkles.

What you need:

150 ml single cream

125 g milk chocolate, roughly chopped

25 g unsalted butter, cut into small pieces

double cream and pink sprinkles, to decorate

1. Put the cream in a small saucepan over a medium heat and slowly bring to boiling point.

2. Add the chocolate and butter and reduce the heat to low. Stir continually until the chocolate and butter have melted and the mixture is smooth.

3. Pour the mixture into 4 small cups or dishes and place in the fridge to set for about 30 minutes.

4. When the mousse has set, spoon a little of the double cream over the top of each pot and decorate with some pink sprinkles.

Step 1

Step 2

Step 4

Ice Cream Sundae

There's only one way to describe this sundae – delicious! It's so yummy it would make a great birthday treat.

10

What you need:

25 g oz chopped mixed
nuts (optional)
8 scoops of vanilla ice cream
grated chocolate and
marshmallows, to serve

Strawberry sauce:
250 g strawberries,
hulled and halved
2 tbsp freshly squeezed
orange juice
2 tbsp caster sugar

1. If you are using the nuts, put them in a dry frying pan and heat for 3 minutes until slightly toasted. Leave to cool.

2. For the strawberry sauce, put the strawberries in a blender with the orange juice and process until smooth.

3. Transfer the mixture to a saucepan and add the sugar. Cook over a medium heat for 10–12 minutes, or until thickened. Leave to cool.

4. Put a spoonful of the strawberry sauce in the bottom of a tall glass. Add two scoops of ice cream and another spoonful of strawberry sauce. Repeat to make 4 sundaes.

5. Sprinkle with the nuts and chocolate. Arrange the marshmallows on top. Serve immediately.

Meringue Clouds

Light and fluffy like clouds, these meringues are topped with a sweet, creamy topping and fresh strawberries.

10

What you need:

4 egg whites
300 g caster sugar
2 tsp white wine vinegar
2 tsp cornflour
300 ml double cream
4 tbsp icing sugar
1 tsp vanilla extract
500 g strawberries, hulled
and halved if large

(!) 1. Preheat the oven to 180°C/350°F/Gas Mark 4. Place a round cutter on top of a sheet of baking paper and carefully trace round it with a pencil. Draw 5 circles on 1 sheet and repeat on another sheet. Put the baking paper, drawn-side down, on the baking sheets.

(!) 2. Put the egg whites in a large bowl, then whisk using an electric hand mixer until the egg whites stand in firm, stiff peaks.

(!) 3. Whisk in the caster sugar a tablespoonful at a time until the mixture is shiny and stiff, then whisk in the vinegar and cornflour.

4. Spoon the mixture onto the circles on the baking paper and make a dip in the centre of each with the back of the spoon.

(!) 5. Bake for 10 minutes, then turn the oven down to 120°C/250°F/Gas Mark ½ and cook for 1 hour. Remove from the oven and leave the meringues to cool a little, then move to a wire rack.

6. Whisk together the cream, icing sugar and vanilla extract in another large bowl until the mixture stands in soft peaks. Spoon the cream into the dips in the meringues and top with strawberries.

Step 3

Step 4

Step 6

My Own Apple Pie

Make apple pies that are extra special by cutting out your initials and adding them to the top of each pie.

10

4   20*   30–35

* plus chilling time

What you need:

225 g plain flour, sifted
pinch of salt
2 tbsp icing sugar
120 g cold unsalted butter,
cut into small pieces
1 egg, separated
1–2 tbsp cold water

Filling:
675 g eating apples, peeled,
halved, cored and thinly
sliced
2 tbsp orange juice
1 tsp ground cinnamon
3 tbsp caster sugar

1. Put the flour, salt and icing sugar in a medium bowl and mix together. Rub in the butter using your fingertips to make a soft buttery mixture. It should look like breadcrumbs.

2. Stir in the egg yolk and water using a wooden spoon, then bring the mixture together with your hands to make a dough. Cover with clingfilm and chill for 30 minutes.

3. For the filling, mix the apple with the orange juice, cinnamon and caster sugar.

4. Preheat the oven to 200°/400°F/Gas Mark 6. Divide the apple mixture between the 4 heatproof dishes. Wet the rim of each dish.

5. Roll out the pastry and cut 4 round tops about 2 cm bigger than the top of the dishes. Top each pie with a pastry round, trim the edges and then press a fork around the edges to seal.

6. Brush each pie with egg white and place the letters on top. Make a slit in the top of each pie, brush with more egg and put on a baking sheet and bake for 30–35 minutes until golden.

Raspberry Jelly

These pretty jellies are so yummy they would be good on their own, but when topped with custard and sprinkles they are simply delicious!

10

6   10*   10

* plus chilling time

What you need:

135 g pack raspberry jelly, cut into small pieces
150 g fresh raspberries (reserve a few to decorate)
sprinkles, to decorate

Custard:
200 ml double cream
2 egg yolks
1 tsp cornflour
1 tsp caster sugar
2 drops vanilla extract

(!) 1. Follow the instructions on the pack to make 600 ml of jelly. Divide the raspberries between 6 x 250 ml small glass dishes.

(!) 2. Pour the liquid jelly onto the raspberries, making sure there is the same amount in each dish. Place in the fridge for 1–2 hours to set.

(!) 3. To make the custard, place the cream in a small saucepan and gradually bring to a boil. In a large heatproof bowl, use a fork to whisk together the egg yolks, cornflour, sugar and vanilla extract until smooth.

(!) 4. Pour the hot cream onto the egg and sugar mixture, whisking all the time with a balloon whisk. Pour the mixture back into the pan and continue whisking over a very gentle heat until it just starts to thicken. Remove from the heat and leave to cool.

5. Pour the cooled custard onto the set jellies and decorate with the sprinkles and reserved raspberries.

Step 3

Step 4

Step 5

Index